flowing in the Way

a contemporary response
to an ancient text

or

just another way
to the *Tao Te Ching*

by j.dubh

Special thanks to Marie for her words of encouragement. This book would still be an idea if not for her.

Thank you to Laura, Beckett, and Sullivan for their love and support.

flowing in the Way: a contemporary response to an ancient text or just another way to the Tao Te Ching by j.dubh

ISBN: 978-1-7753219-0-3

naught noteworthy books
printed and bound by lulu.com

One who learns
is a learner
One who knows
is a knower
One who teaches
is a teacher
And one who flows
is a flow-er
and a flower
Because the act of flowing
is a kind of blossoming
into that which is beautiful
in the world
and the self

the flow-er
j.dubh

flowing in the Way: A Response to the Tao Te Ching

There are a great many concise, insightful, and beautifully translated versions of the *Tao Te Ching*. This is not one of them. Rather, this book is meant to be inspired by reflection upon those many translations, reflection on the Tao itself, and interpretation of the Way in my own life. While each of the eighty-one chapters of this book is closely related to each of the eighty-one chapters of the *Tao Te Ching*, each of my chapters is a meditative response to the text rather than a translation of any kind. If you are indeed looking for an actual translation of the original text, please look elsewhere – I have some suggestions for some excellent sources at the end of this book, for example.

A Disclaimer: I am not a Taoist scholar. I am simply one who flows in the Way, or tries to, every day. I am a teacher and artist, and as such, my life is filled with opportunities to learn, interpret, share, and create. *flowing in the Way* as an idea and text has been with me for over a decade. At this point, I feel I can share it with anyone interested in seeing the Way as it may be felt by me, a non-scholar in a non-academic sense. Taoism and understanding the Way does not require training, initiation, or guidance. For many, it is often discovered and investigated in a very personal way. This book is meant to support those interested in the Tao.

Tao Te Ching may be translated as the *Classic Text of the Way and of Virtue* (or *Power*, but I prefer Virtue). In short, while there are other books of importance to Taoists, this is the root text. Its perceived author, Lao Tzu, is likely to have merely collected these bits of wisdom (there is much debate on that) to create the story of the Way. The text itself is divided between the *Book of Tao*, chapters one through thirty-seven, and the *Book of Te*, chapters thirty-eight through eighty-one. I have not chosen to make such a division as this is not a literal translation.

Some notes on language before we go too far. In my attempt to envision the text and the Tao, I have made some deliberate choices with regard to specific words. First, rather than Tao or Dao, I prefer to use Way. Tao may be translated as way, path, route, or any sentiment that suggests direction toward destination. As an English speaker, the word *way* with its connotations of direction alongside method of thinking as well as system of belief carries with it a wonderfully vague yet understandable sense of itself. And for me, that is also a great definition of Tao, as wonderfully vague yet still completely certain, still knowable.

Many translations also refer to the master or sage when referencing one who practices the teachings of Tao. I in no way see myself as reflected in either of these terms. I dare say a great many of us would simply baulk at such a designation no matter our level of experience or proficiency in any field. I have instead chosen to focus on the use of *one*, as in one who flows in the Way, because to me this feels more inclusive and inviting to all levels of experience and understanding. At times, especially in the latter half of the text, I have resorted to the use of you. I did consciously attempt to avoid this when possible simply because the use of that pronoun engenders a feeling of *should* along with it. I do not believe that the *Tao Te Ching* is a shouldy document, although I do understand that many may see it that way. I hope that a sense of *one may do this* or *one may see that* is conveyed rather than you should do this or you must do that.

The use of the word *flow* is important to my version as well. As you may already know, and will certainly see in my version of the *Tao Te*

Ching, Taoists have long venerated water for its wonderful combination of patient strength and superior flexibility. Water attains these qualities by being in flow. Water is gentle whenever possible, but vigorous by circumstance. When one attempts to be *flowing in the Way,* one tries to become as water toward others and for the self.

The concept of flow, as it has been described by the psychologist Mihaly Csikszentmihalyi, is a state of absorbed concentration. And this is a connotation I wish to conjure as well. I see the work of Csikszentmihalyi as closely parallel to a central tenet of Taoism and *flowing in the Way*. It relates to the Taoist notion of *doing without action*, or rather doing without struggle against. His conceptualization of being in flow, or *being in the zone* as it may be termed, is to my mind the absolute peak of mindfulness and engagement with the Way. If you haven't heard of Csikszentmihalyi and his work on flow, I very much recommend you check it out.

Finally, and quite naturally, I have removed any masculine pronouns in my response to the many translations I have worked with over the years. To be sure, I recognize the use of *he* and *him* and *his* in translations of the past as referring directly to the historical reality of the text and the time of the translation, surely a time of male dominance across most cultures. If I may, I would suggest that one should not avoid or be offended by masculine focused word use in any translation given the continued accepted use of such pronouns at the time of translation. Many engaging translations do utilize male pronouns, but there is so much more to be gained by overlooking this flaw and by seeing the deeper meanings presented by each of the translating authors. Now with that said, it was not at all difficult for me to avoid these pronouns, so why not do so? The Way itself has no gender, or rather, it is both genders in one.

If this will be your first reading of the *Tao Te Ching* in any form, I strongly encourage you to also examine various translations and other interpretations as well. As you will see, Tao or the Way, is difficult to name, to define, and should be seen unrestrained by the confines of language to be fully enjoyed and understood. My words may indeed not resonate with you while the words of another may ring true. If you have some experience with the Way, I hope you find my work here refreshing, renewing, and reinvigorating along your own journey toward flowing in the Way.

A very brief primer for Taoism and the Way

The eighty-one chapters of the *Tao Te Ching* or *Dao De Jing* (as it is pronounced) are believed to be accumulated works of the new forms of Chinese philosophy and wisdom prevalent in the sixth through fourth century BCE. It is also believed, yet much debated, that these chapters are the singular work of one man, Lao Tzu (Laozi, or Lao Tse as well). This name may be translated as Old Master and so some contend that rather than writing each of the chapters himself, a sage or master collected these poetic epistles and presented them to those that sought knowledge. In any case, the text and its various potential interpretations have been the focus of most scholarship rather than their origins. Some excavations and further research have revealed the possibility of additional chapters, and there is a number of English translations which date back to at least the mid 1800s. While all of this may be of interest to readers who are new to Taoism, it is not required reading. The key to embracing Taoism, the Way, and the *Tao Te*

Ching is finding a text which speaks to you as the reader. While much has been written on the history and evolution of the interpretation of the text, my work has very little to do with any of the history of the text and seeks instead to inform the present.

In Zen, a form of Buddhism which was heavily influenced by Taoism, there is a wonderful word that I like to borrow which describes how best to see the text of the *Tao Te Ching* and especially the text of my book, whether you are new to Taoism or not. The word is *shoshin* and it means *beginner's mind*. In Taoism as in Zen, there is a call to openness that suggests one should enter into all things with the mind of a child, to see things anew whenever possible. Without preconceptions, a beginner approaches something with an earnest eagerness which others seemingly more knowledgeable have left behind and possibly forgotten. And as you will see by reading any version of the *Tao Te Ching*, or as you may already have experienced, there is a difference between collecting information and truly knowing. Too often, I would suggest, the ability to collect and store data in one's head is prized above the simple act of knowing, a much less cerebral and much more personal act.

It is with this in mind that I leave you with this (hopefully) brief introduction to the text of *flowing in the Way*. Read with the mind of a beginner. If I may suggest, try to read only one chapter at a time. Allow the meaning of it to be absorbed and understood as only you may perceive it. And, if you find yourself intrigued and thirsty for more, look to the many others who have written beautifully and deeply on the nature of Tao. The journey of true discovery is measured only steps taken, not in metres nor in millennia.

j.dubh
March, 2018

flowing in the Way

one: *What is the Way?*

There is a way
of living,
of being,
of seeing,
and knowing

But,
it is a way
that cannot be taught, created, or concealed
it can only be
found, felt, and embraced

It is the Way
that is everything
and nothing
in which all happens
in which all exists

But the Way
is nothing
in that it is everything
though it cannot be touched
though it cannot be seen

The Way is the everything
that ever exists
and it is the nothing
of all that has existed

In the world of
all that may be
and all that has been
flows the Way
for the two are indistinguishable

two: *Absence*

Often the absence of one
implies the presence of another
but that is not true
when flowing in the Way

When one sees beauty
one concedes ugliness
When one praises goodness
one acknowledges evil
When one sighs for melody
one dismisses noise
When one triumphs past difficulty
one degrades simple deeds

Flowing in the Way
means acknowledging presence
The presence of all things
without bias or predisposition

Flowing in the Way
means acceptance of
the high and low
without action
without preference

three: *Inaction*

Flowing in the Way
means to flow like water
around obstacles
wearing down barriers
with time
and patience

When one acts to contend
one will be met with opposition
so
act with purpose
but not desire
or
seek no action at all
and find purpose
in being still

four: *Unending*

The Way has no end
because there is no beginning

The Way cannot be created
and so not destroyed

It comes before us
and so remains after

Is of nature
and beyond it

Thus, it will fill you
whether you know it
or not

five: *Neutrality*

The Way is like nature
it is neutral in all things
takes no sides
and fights no battles

And yet, nature
and the Way
always remain
no matter what
harm is imposed

When one flows in the Way
one becomes neutral
and, like nature,
is never exhausted

six: *Experience*

There are many things you already know
The Way flows through your experience
Trust in yourself
and all that you’ve done
you will find a way
even if you don’t yet know
the Way

There’s no deeper resource
than yourself
as source material

seven: *Service*

The Way has purpose
because it does not serve itself

Flowing in the Way
means finding a way to serve
those other than the self

In service to others
one may find purpose

eight: *Water*

To know the Way
one must understand
the elegance of water

Water flows
downhill
along the easiest path
bringing life
and smoothing
its own way
with patient tenacity

That is why it is called
Flowing in the Way
It means being like water
being adaptable and
seeking stillness

nine: *Accumulation*

There is no reason to accumulate
when one flows in the Way

Gathering materials means they must be stored
What use are accumulated things
if they are not used?
What benefit is stockpiled wealth
if there is no worthy purchase?
Why hold on to things
when life itself may not be held?

Flowing in the Way
means living with enough
and knowing when to let go

ten: *Acceptance*

To know the Way
one must be accepting
of the self
of others

To become accepting
one must nurture
themselves and others

To become nurturing
one must be open
to the self and others

Too often we believe
that openness leads to the rest
But true openness
only comes from
accepting then nurturing

And to flow with the Way
one must give and embrace
without expectation of recompense

eleven: *Use*

The usefulness of a thing
is not always determined by what we see

A cup finds use
in what it can hold
Walls and a roof find their use
in what they can protect
A book finds its meaning
when the reader imbues the words
A tucked wing finds its purpose
when extended in flight

And so
one who flows in the Way
may be of use
for what is unseen
by others
or even, sometimes
by the self

twelve: *Overload*

In many ways
we seek too much
of everything
sounds ever loud
colours so vivid
maximum experience
the optimal, the ultimate,
unbelievable, irreplaceable

But when one flows in the Way
one sees with clarity
and without regard
for extremes

In this way
one seeks balance
one finds beauty
in all things
small and large

thirteen: *Self*

Much of the world seeks
to measure us in artificial ways
We are praised
We are blamed
We are raised
We are shamed

But when one flows in the Way
one disregards both that which seeks
to elevate
and that which seeks
to devalue
for neither is a true measure
of the self

fourteen: *Unseen*

The Way is unseen
because it is in all things
and nothing at once

Because it is unseen
it cannot be held
or withdrawn
it cannot be defined
or derided

So to flow in the Way
one must find
the essence
of all things
surrounding and inside
the self
and feel for
the continuity of now

fifteen: *Learning*

Flowing in the Way
one may learn many things
The first may be that
knowing the Way
is something
that can be learned
but is rarely taught

Those that have come
to know the Way
do so because they
attend, investigate, scrutinize
but then reserve judgment
Because they know that
that which they do not know
far exceeds that which
they will ever understand

sixteen: *Empty*

The Way is harder to see
when we are full
of information and opinion
built for us by others
clung to by our ego

To find the Way
one must become empty
of information and opinion
built for us by others
clung to by our ego

This is also the way of nature
All living things in the natural world
except for us
shed themselves
of all that they do not need
to flourish in the moment

Learning to empty
to recede and then renew
such as the natural world
is the path to the Way

seventeen: *Leaders*

Those that learn to lead
by flowing in the Way
do so without need
for recognition or admiration

The best leaders create
a belief in others
that they themselves
have lead the way

eighteen: *Consequence*

When one forgets the Way
one may fall victim
to persuasive authority
and flattering media
while still believing
one flows in the Way

When one becomes aware
of mistaken loyalty
to nations, to brands, to ideals
one simply must find their way
back to nature, to harmony
and to the flow of the Way

or the consequence
is chaos

nineteen: *Cleanse*

So much of knowledge
is based in cultural artifice
So much of what we know
is intellectual clutter
and not essential to living
in simplicity and peace

So many of our habits
are cultural reproduction
and provide little in the way
of comfort and solace
when examined with clarity

Those who flow in the Way
cleanse whenever possible
false knowledge
and reckless desire

twenty: *Wanderlust*

Those who flow in the Way
often appear lost, confused, or even foolish
to people possessed with purpose
living within the cultural norm

One who flows in the Way
embraces a wanderlust
in learning
in work
in travel
living spare
and finding stillness

Wandering as a way of life
means not fearing the future
and not lamenting the past
It means following the natural flow
of circumstance presented before you
and facing each moment
on the merits of the challenge
each event presents

twenty-one: *Beneath*

The Way lives in harmony
with all things
because it lies beneath
all things
and takes no acclaim

To find the Way
one must then look deeply
into all things
into all peoples
into the self
accepting them all
for what they are

twenty-two: *Home*

The world is a hostile place
in which a home
can be difficult to find

Those who flow in the Way
have found a home
within the chaos
of daily life
by accepting
the world as it is

Seek to empty
avoid contention
embrace change and renewal
and you will find
a quiet island
in the swirling world
to call home

twenty-three: *Language*

The natural world speaks very little
in a language of communication
The natural world feels and responds
is harsh and calm, loud and quiet
but its moods do not last for long

Flowing in the Way means
being attune to the world
in ways other than language
and realizing that harmony comes
when words fail to be
one's singular form
of communication with the world
and the self

twenty-four: *Humility*

Prominence is conspicuous
Promotion is propaganda
Pride is conceit

Those who flow in the Way
are self-effacing
rather than self-aggrandizing
because those who are weak
seek to claim their place
in the construct of society
while those that are humble
seek only to construct
a place in society
for harmony

twenty-five: *Limitless*

The Way has no limitations
and is in all things
and yet has no form
or meaning or name

It is called ‘the Way’
because our language
requires labels for things

But, as with nature
it would exist without
a name
and still be
the way of the world
limitless
even if we were not
to name it

twenty-six: *Calm*

Urgency is the way of calamity
Deliberation is the Way of calm

Even after fretting over the trivial
during the light of day
we will all find sleep
by the darkened night

Flowing in the Way
means greeting
celerity with consideration

twenty-seven: *Footprint*

Moving through the world
one must leave no trace
upon the earth

Moving in the world
one may leave a mark
upon its people

Flowing in the Way
means leaving no work
behind for others to complete

Flowing in the Way
means one may leave works
behind for others to continue

twenty-eight: *Contrast*

Strength is born from contrasts
and the balance of opposing forces

Become male knotted with female
enter the dark to see the light
empower the self
against the chaos of the world

One who intertwines opposites
tradition and innovation
learning and habit
introspection with culture
becomes strong
in the Way
and the world

twenty-nine: *Ambition*

Society tells us that without ambition
we will be nothing
but it is those that seek
to possess that indeed
own nothing

The natural world
is shaped by the Way
The artificial world
is fashioned by the self

It is a mistake to believe
that you can force change
without damaging
the world
and the self

thirty: *Violence*

Power begotten through violence
is lost through violence
All who have conquered
have themselves been conquered
It is hubris
that forgets this simple truth

A leader who flows in the Way
will act out of necessity
empower through agency
and engage with discretion
the violence of opposition
secure in the knowledge
that any act of violence
must be answered for
in time

thirty-one: *Force*

Force is a tool of violence
Its use creates only fear and hate
and it is used to gain power
only through destruction
Those who flow in the Way
do not seek to gain
and labour only
to create

Weapons are tools of force
Their use creates only fear and hate
and they are used to gain power
only through devastation

Those who flow in the Way
take no delight
in the art of weaponry
because their creation
can have but one end

thirty-two: *Form*

The Way is not restricted
to any shape
and so cannot be controlled
in any form

If a leader were to find
a form of the Way
which he claimed to control
he would soon realize
that which was being controlled
would be him

Either harmony would result
from the Way guiding him
or he would soon be relieved
of power for being misguided
in his perception of control

The Way only takes form in use
and once used
returns to formlessness

thirty-three: *Acquiesce*

Those who come to
flow in the Way
do so by acquiescing

Much of what may have been learned
prior to knowing the Way
will turn out to be false
and will be difficult
to turn away from

thirty-four: *Control*

In nature and the Way
there is no false
belief in control

Nature and the Way
provide for all things
but seek only harmony

Without intent
without expectation
and without recompense

To flow in the Way
one must surrender
all aspiration to control

thirty-five: *People*

If one provides substance
to people
one may find people
with whom to walk

If one flows in the Way
one will find
all the world
walks with them

thirty-six: *Opposition*

Moving through our world
one will often meet with opposition
But when flowing in the Way
one does not seek conflict
and so a problem arises

Those who seek power are gluttonous
so feed them
Those driven by desire are voracious
so flatter them
They will gorge themselves
They will grow arrogant
And they will fall

On the path to avoiding conflict
walk on stones of subtlety

thirty-seven: *Desire*

Desires are wants
that cloak themselves in need

Abandon desire
it has no purpose in nature
or the self

Harmony is the antithesis of desire
They cannot coexist
And with harmony
one becomes quiet
one finds tranquility
a state devoid
of desire

thirty-eight: *Reproduction*

The false hierarchies of society
maintain themselves through
cultural reproduction

Nature maintains itself
in the harmony of flow

Cultural reproduction acts
to enforce ritual acceptance
of unnatural laws
upon the earth
and all living things

Nature acts to maintain itself
with balance for all living things

The rules of culture change
The laws of nature subsist
People act with reason
Nature acts without action
Societies rise and fall
But the Way of nature remains

thirty-nine: *Foundations*

One may build a life
on the foundations of nature
and the Way
Leaders may build society
on the foundations of people
and nature

One who builds a life
in nature will flourish
One who builds a life
from nature will find folly
For to live in nature
is the way to harmony
But to live from nature
is the way to ruin

And so
A leader who builds a society
from foundations of a valued people
living in flow with nature
will lead with humility and harmony
But
A leader who suppresses a people
will erode those foundations
in hubris and vanity
leading to humiliation and defeat

forty: *Cycles*

The Way travels in cycles
forever beginning and ending
so that there is no start
and no end
only flow

forty-one: *Flowing*

Upon learning of the Way
one may have a variety of reactions
One may scoff and scorn
in fear of looking foolish
One may deride and disparage
in fear of a contested belief
One may look upon it with interest
briefly, and then move along

In any case, the Way still flows
though it does nothing to attract
It is plain
It is simple
It is bland
It is meek

Those who flow in the Way
seem to wander without purpose
And, in the end
there is no glorious reward

The Way merely is
and those who find its flow
seek only to be

forty-two: *Sensing*

The mind cannot comprehend
the Way
The Way is found
by sensing

Nature does not think
but rather it senses
change, growth, decay
feeling its way from
season to season

Flowing in the Way
requires sensing
and thinking is often
the enemy of sensation

So,
shut down the mind
and feel your way

forty-three: *Erosion*

Erosion is a process
of water and wind
patiently tempering the stone

Erosion works with natural flow
It is action without action
It is nature’s transformative power

Those who flow in the Way
use erosive patience to make change

forty-four: *Contentment*

Greatness requires a cost
that those who flow in the Way
simply refuse to pay

Great knowledge means ignoring
other pursuits due to specialization
Great wealth means ignoring
other people through segregation

Great power comes
at the cost of others
But great contentment comes
at no cost
other than glory

forty-five: *Quiet*

Perfection pursued is incomplete
but embracing the imperfect
makes one whole

Truth pursued will always contradict
but embracing the unknown
makes one wise

All things are undone in time
and so, be quiet
be calm, and wait
for all things will be undone
and then done again

forty-six: *Sickness*

When a people flow in the Way
They can be found cultivating the earth together
And comforting one another
When a people lose the Way
They can be found marching the streets together
In conflict with an Other

It is a sickness
that can grow within us
luring us into desire
forming a taste for attaining
into a thirst to be only quenched by more

It is a sickness
to forget contentment
for which the only cure
comes not from without
but from within

forty-seven: *Less*

One need not venture into the world
to know its colour
its taste
its smell

One can know less
of the world
by staying at home
But one can learn much
of the self
by turning within

The world will not miss you
But you should not miss yourself

forty-eight: *Forget*

The pursuit of knowledge
involves daily learning
Flowing in the Way
involves daily forgetting
While there is much that may be learned
there is much that should be forgotten

The world is continuously built
through accumulation
of information mistaken as knowledge
misunderstood to be wisdom

By forgetting the excess
and ignoring the unfounded
one comes to know less
save for that which matters most

forty-nine: *Needs*

One who flows in the Way
becomes indistinguishable from the whole
and so the needs of the world
become the needs of the one

Towards equality, one treats all equally
Towards peace, one is always kind
Towards justice, one is trustworthy
Towards harmony, one nurtures others

One who flows in the Way
cares for the needs of nature
as nature cares for us
without bias, cause, or conviction
One cares simply because
one needs to be cared for

fifty: *Death*

One may be filled with life
or emptied by death
there is but a simple choice

Those who flow in the Way
are not emptied by fear
because fear is a death repeated

If one makes a place for fear
one makes a place for death
If one makes a place for only life
death has no place in them
so fear is lost
and life is full

fifty-one: *Nurturing*

When one flows in the Way
one seeks to nurture
all things and all people

service is the most honourable
of professions
because one finds purpose
in use
And being of use
completes them

fifty-two: *Childish*

Those who flow in the Way
seek to be like a child
for it is children who see
the world anew
and with respectful awe

it is children who seek
to be taught
rather than teach
it is children who show
respect rather than arrogance
it is children who play
rather than toil

so, seek to be a child
be open and wonder
let yourself be small
and seek not to be greater
than you are

fifty-three: *Challenge*

Flowing in the Way
is not a challenge
for the path is simple
and well travelled

But challenge has its lure
We seek a difficulty
to prove something
to others and the self

But those who flow in the Way
have found that challenge
is a conceit used by the self
to find worth above others

It is a false way
to value oneself
better than another
by challenges met

fifty-four: *Empathy*

Find empathy for yourself
and harmony grows within you
Empathize with those closest to you
and relationships will strengthen
Empathize with those in your community
and you become a spoke in the wheel of unity
Empathize with those around the world
and you become one with the Way

Harmony starts with love and empathy
for the self
and spreads out to the world

fifty-five: *Grace*

Those who flow in the Way
seek to move upon the earth
with grace

Graceful movements are made mindfully
they are not rushed
they are not made in competition

Moving gracefully through the world
allows one to be soft yet certain
vigorous yet controlled
sensuous yet unassuming

Moving with excesses brings calamity
Moving with grace brings calm

fifty-six: *Proselytising*

Those who flow in the Way
often do so rather quietly

Coming to the Way
is a singular journey
and though one may share
a knowledge of the Way
no two paths will be the same

Each of us is but one
So be reserved in your belief
and accept that all of us
are on our own journeys
toward our own ends

fifty-seven: *Reaction*

Those who flow in the Way
choose not to control others
The act of control
fosters a reaction
Yet taking no action
leaves a void

In the absence of control
people will seek
to fill this void
with collaboration
for we cannot survive alone

Without an external rule of law
People will seek to rule themselves

fifty-eight: *Perhaps*

Those who flow in the Way
fear not an end
because they see
that there is no end

Those who seek to rule
and control the acts of others
speak of desperate ends
as the result of action
as the result of taking no action

But those who flow in the Way
suggest that
perhaps
there is no end
and so no forever despair

Perhaps there is dark
and then there is light
Perhaps there is calamity
and then there is fortune

And knowing there is no end
frees us from fear
and from control

fifty-nine: *Restraint*

Many people see contention
as the only route to attainment
but those who flow in the Way
see restraint as a route to harmony

What can be gained by taking
will not be held from being taken
But what may be attained by acquiescence
will be held through agreement

sixty: *Demons*

There are demons that haunt us each
Our own monsters roaming
the passages of the mind

These are creatures
that feed on disquiet
But when one flows in the Way
these demons in turn lose theirs

While they will be ever-present
their ability to harm us and others
is ever increasingly diminished
making a peaceful accord possible

sixty-one: *Submission*

To many the idea of submission
is an abhorrent sign of weakness
but when we submit
we often relinquish ourselves
from the control of desire

The first act in regaining control
for ourselves is submitting
to the reality that we ourselves
are often not in control

sixty-two: *Impartial*

To flow in the Way
one must become impartial
for anything that is celebrated
may then be defamed
and any intrigue
could lead to innovation

And so
those who flow in the Way
seek only to embrace
those whom have found their Way
and judge not the belief of others

sixty-three: *Small*

All things may be managed
when they are small
All things may be understood
when they are small

Those who flow in the Way
examine facets to consider complexity
and explore the possibility of an element
to become part of a larger whole

All things that are now seemingly infinite
began as but a grain
And all things that are small
have the potential to be great

sixty-four: *Care*

Those who flow in the Way
take care at the beginning
and at the end

In the beginning
it is natural to nurture
to foster growth
and facilitate blossoming

But care is also taken at the end
when it is time to return
For the only true way
to fail in this life
is to leave without sharing
that which has left
its mark on you

There is a reason
that death may be named
passing on

sixty-five: *Subtlety*

Though many see them in contradiction
there is power in subtlety
One may gain influence
through bold strokes
But one may gain enmity
in the same action

Flowing in the Way
means engaging the subtle
so as to find one's place
without cost to others

Within the subtle
there is contemplation,
collaboration, and calm

sixty-six: *Following*

Knowing how to follow
is the key to becoming a leader
For being worthy of the title master
means first a time of service

So it is that sometimes
those that flow in the Way
may be seen as wise
after years of practice

But this is due to perception
because the reality is
that the Way is the master
and we have merely found
our way in following

sixty-seven: *Importance*

There are many
who seek to be
of importance
in this life

But to be important
one must become distinctive
one must be separate
from the rest
and the world

But one so separate
will not endure

Those who flow in the Way
seek to be unimportant
in union and harmony
with others and the world
and so one shall endure
through compassion and restraint

sixty-eight: *Compassion*

Compassion allows one to protect
and at once be protected
Compassion builds empathy for
others and the self
building understanding
within and without

Command through
authority, aggression, and fear
may certainly allow one to win
But those who flow in the Way
do not hunger for such a prize
that may be won so

sixty-nine: *Disaster*

For those who flow in the Way
there is no worse disaster
than misunderstanding

Misunderstanding others
leads to offense, contention, and conflict
Misunderstanding the self
leads to anxiety, confusion, and injury

Flowing in the Way
one deepens understanding
through restraint
moving with subtlety
seeking to be unimportant
and acting with others
and the self compassionately
This is the way of harmony

seventy: *Individuality*

Flowing in the Way
is possible for any and all
But my journey is my own
My words may be understood
My actions may be reproduced
but no other will find
the exact same meaning
and so I find myself
in the great flow
that is the Way

Harmony is built and maintained
from the strength of diversity
not the frailty of
singular invocation

seventy-one: *Limitation*

It is a strength to know one's limits
for each of us has boundaries
that may at times be challenged
but must at all times be respected

Ignoring one's limits
is the source of ill health
Respecting one's limits
is the way to healing

seventy-two: *Revolution*

Revolt comes upon a people
when they no longer fear
a fate worse than that
which exists upon them now

Revolution comes to the self
when we no longer fear
a fate worse than that
which we have wrought upon ourselves

There is freedom in knowing
that we are only what we make
ourselves to be

So, measure yourself
by no other rule
than that which you make
and you too will find
a way to revolution

seventy-three: *Time*

There is no force
with the power of time
All things bend to its will

And yet, so many seek
to cheat time of its due
So many seek to gain seconds
save minutes, store days
But this is folly

Those who flow in the Way
seek to partner with time
acting in harmony with its wishes
for it is not an enemy
unless one sees it as such

Time has a plan for all ages
and knowing such purpose
gives joy to each day

seventy-four: *Judgment*

When we do not understand
we often offer our judgment
based on only what we know
This is flawed reasoning

Seek to understand
rather than judge
for those who would speak ill
of the carpenter
oft injure themselves
when presented with hammer and nail

seventy-five: *Without*

Because there are those that have
There must be those that have not
Because there is that which we value
There must be that which we do not
But those who flow in the Way
seek to be without
Without the want to have
there is no pain of desire
Without a belief in value
there is no judgment of belief

Without regard for one's life
above that of another
one can live in harmony with all

seventy-six: *Softness*

To many, strength is measured
as a degree of toughness
the ability to hold firm
and the fortitude to remain rigid

But this is not the way of nature

In nature, that which is stiff
lacks water, lacks life
and is easily broken

In nature, that which is strong
is filled with water, with life
and will bend without breaking

Those that flow in the Way
know tenderness is strength
and that to be hard
is to be inflexible and dead

seventy-seven: *Give*

In nature, too many predators
means too little prey
and so the predators will starve
until an equilibrium returns

It is not so with humanity

We will take until there is very little
and then invent new ways to take
from that very little which remains
with no sense of equilibrium

But those that flow in the Way
choose to give
without expectation
whenever possible
because they know
the cost of taking

seventy-eight: *Yield*

That which is soft
may overcome
that which is hard
through determined yielding

Those that flow in the Way
are like water
and will find the path
of least resistance
by seeming to yield
to hardened obstacles

But with time and equanimity
passing over, around, and through
each obstacle results in
a softening of edges
a deepening of chasm
and an opening of a way through

Yielding is the only way
to truly overcome

seventy-nine: *Reconciliation*

In all of life
there will be conflict
And at the end
there will be a time
to reconcile

Those that flow in the Way
know that this is the moment
to accept less than may be afforded
For justice seeks a price
while harmony welcomes accord
And yielding to the grace of peace
truly comes a little cost

eighty: *Dwell*

It is natural
that one may travel
to see the wide world
from time to time
But those who flow in the Way
seek to dwell
in their communities

One cannot look too often to the horizon
without turning one's back on home
And so, seek to dwell
where it is you reside
know it intimately
since that is the place
that you may change most
and that will most change you

eight-one: *Flowing in the Way*

To flow in the Way
one must above all
seek service
to nature
to others
and to the self

Wealth will not bring contentment
Learning does not always bring wisdom
But giving of the self brings purpose
while meaning is found in the footprint
one leaves on others and the world

when there is no enemy within,
the enemies outside cannot harm you.

African Proverb

first hold peace within yourself,
only then can you bring it to others.

Thomas a Kempis

Writing these chapters has been part of my journey. Like many, I write to understand things about myself, and the world. I have learned much. I have unlearned even more. There is a balance that must be found between knowledge and knowing.

j.dubh

selected source material
& suggested reading:

Ball, Pamela. The essence of Tao. Arcturus Publishing Limited, 2016.

Blakney, R.B. The way of life Lao Tzu: a new translation of the Tao Te Ching. New American Library, 1955.

Cheng, François, and Fabienne Verdier. In love with the way: Chinese poems of the Tang Dynasty. Shambhala, 2002.

Csikszentmihalyi, Mihaly. Finding flow: the psychology of engagement with everyday life. Basic Books, 2008.

Cleary, Thomas. The essential Tao: an initiation into the heart of taoism through the authentic Tao Te Ching and the inner teachings of Chuang-Tzu. Harper, 2000.

Deng, Ming-Dao. 365 Tao: daily meditations. HarperSanFrancisco, 2006.

Deng, Ming-Dao. Everyday Tao: living with balance and harmony. HarperSanFrancisco, 1996.

Hoff, Benjamin, and Ernest H. Shepard. The Tao of Pooh. Penguin Books, 1986.

Hoff, Benjamin. The te of Piglet. Penguin Books, 1993.

Laozi, and Stephen Mitchell. Tao te ching: a new English version. HarperPerennial, 2006.

Laozi, and Stephen Mitchell. Tao te ching. Frances Lincoln Limited, 2009.

Laozi, and Timothy Freke. Lao Tzus Tao te ching. Piatkus, 1999.

Laozi, et al. Tao te ching. Vega, 2002.

Levering, Miriam. Zen inspirations: essential meditations and texts. Chartwell Books, Inc., 2013.

Snelling, John. Way of Buddhism. Thorsons, 2001.

Towler, Solala. Chi energy of happiness. Andrews McMeel, 2002.

Towler, Solala. Chi: energy of harmony. Andrews McMeel, 2002.

Wong, Eva. The Shambhala guide to Taoism. Shambhala, 1997.

www.ingramcontent.com/pod-product-compliance
Ingram Content Group UK Ltd.
Pitfield, Milton Keynes, MK11 3LW, UK
UKHW020220250726
13967UKWH00001B/102